As an Occupational Ther... ist, I have found
inspiration for The Melt... ...orking
with families of childre...
their behaviours when ... d.
This means that meltd...
being naughty but a res...
either physically, emotionally or from a ...
perspective.

Children typically go into any or all of the following survival behaviours due to fear:
Fight: exploding like a volcano, which can be verbal or physical aggression.
Flight: running away and/or hiding.
Freeze: avoiding something that is overwhelming by passively ignoring or becoming defiant and digging their heels in.
Dissociation: disconnect, detached, daydreaming
Shutdown: loss of tone, sleepy, collapse

It is important to try to understand the reason for the meltdown and help parents to support their children with sensory and nurture strategies.

I hope these little books will help you.

Linda Plowden - OT, Therapy Space Bristol Ltd

Nathan was in the swimming pool with lots of other children, but he didn't want to play with any of them.

Danny was Nathan's older brother and it was his birthday party. They were playing a game called 'Shark Attack!' Danny was pretending to be a shark and the other children were trying not to get caught!

But Nathan kept running around the pool and dive-bombing everyone.

Their dad, said, “I want you to stop that right now!” But Nathan wasn’t listening. He dive-bombed Jenny. Her mouth filled with water and she started to cough and cry.

Then he dive-bombed Ashley, sending a wave of water slapping into his face. “Stop it!” shouted Ashley as he tried to grab Nathan. But Nathan didn’t like being touched. He was slippery like an eel and he wriggled free.

Dad was angry, and when Nathan climbed out of the pool, he tried to catch him. But Nathan was fast. He poked out his tongue and he ran away.

It was time to get changed and everybody was angry with Nathan.

“Why did you have to dive-bomb us?” asked Jenny.
“I was just having fun!”

But he knew that he wasn’t really having fun at all. He felt bad that he had ruined their game. His mum was really cross with him.

Nathan spent ages getting changed. He hadn't dried himself properly and he hated the feeling of all the sticky clothes on his skin.

All the other children had to wait for him and his mum asked, "Why does it always take you so long?"

When they were changed they all sat around the table. It was covered in plates of sandwiches, sausage rolls and all kinds of biscuits.

Nathan watched enviously as Danny unwrapped his presents. It seemed to go on forever!

He couldn't keep still. He started running about and stuffing food into his mouth.

"Calm down, Nathan!" said mum
But he couldn't.

When the lights were dimmed his dad came in carrying Danny's birthday cake. The candles lit up the room and everybody sang, 'Happy Birthday.'

Danny blew out the candles and
everybody clapped and cheered.

Everybody except Nathan.

He took a long look at the delicious chocolate cake and, before he had had time to think, he had dug his hands right into it!

All the other children looked on with horror as he grabbed a big chunk of cake and shoved it in his mouth.

Danny yelled,
"I hate you!
Why do you
have to ruin
everything!"

Nathan was shocked

Nathan felt awful. He hated behaving badly. It made him feel terrible

But somehow he couldn't help it.

Mum started crying and left the room.

"I'm so embarrassed," said Nathan's mum. "Sometimes I don't know what to do!"

"Maybe I can help you?" said one of the other mums. "My son always got so over-excited and jealous of his sister when it was her birthday!"

“Perhaps you can give me some tips on what to do?”

“Yes, of course I can!”

So, next week at Finn's swimming party, Nathan didn't feel he had to join in with the pool games.

They let him jump into the pool as much as he wanted and he loved diving for coins.

The feeling of the water pressed against his skin made him feel calmer.

It was much easier in the changing rooms as his mum remembered to bring talcum powder to help the clothes slip over his damp skin.

They would let him spend as much time as he needed drying himself.

They knew that if he became upset, they could give him something to chew. Dried mango and bubble gum were his favourites.

TALC

He loved joining in when the children made balloon animals.

Blowing the balloons made him feel calm, and when Nathan was calm he felt happy.

So, when they went home, Nathan was relaxed and smiling.

“Did you have fun today?” Rowan and Paula asked him.

“I had a great time!” said Nathan. “I can’t wait for the next party!”

Postscript

Nathan is a sensory seeker and is impulsive. He has ADHD and Sensory Processing Disorder (SPD). He loves to "crash and bang", which is a proprioceptive seeking behaviour, i.e. jumping into the pool. Children like him also love to swim under water but cannot cope with lessons.

He is hyperactive, overexcited and loud. When children are noisy it usually indicates that they are frightened. He dive bombs other children in the pool as he cannot cope with the structured games. He is also jealous that it is his brother's birthday and all the attention is on him. He creates situations where he gets good or bad reactions from adults as it is better than no attention at all.

He also struggles with the sensory overload of feeling wet and not being able to get his clothes on quickly after swimming.